Between Earth and Sky

Poetry by
Lou Faiel-Dattilo

2nd Tier Publishing

Published by:
  2nd Tier Publishing
  501 Wimberley Oaks Dr
  Wimberley, TX 78676-4671, U.S.A.

ISBN 978-0-578-10407-2

Cover and book design by Dan Gauthier, 2nd Tier Publishing

for
Sandy Bartlett,
my partner of 32 years

That there is Poetry
Sings of something
More than
eyes on the

                  Ground.

Lifting them up from
Graveled walks suggesting
Seasonal

                  Streams.

Past Sun Rays shining
Through the open Cedars,

                  Sky!

Contents

Heaven

Humanity

Earth

Heaven

SPACE

Those whirling maelstroms
of vibrant fiery
energy
the whirligigs
of gaseous explosions
so vast
they spill out of the
minds of greater men
than I
yet so far away
and so at winter night
sitting
We conceive them
charming strings of
jewels
or queens on thrones
or bears or fish
or archers

THE NIGHT AND THE QUIET DARKNESS

the night and the quiet
darkness
surround me
astounding this
private hour with
the space of
a thousand
star-system
moments
and here there is
no one to
praise or blame
and dreams
break thru
with insidious
wisdom

MOON

the Moon
and Jupiter so big to her left and south
she's so reading-by-it bright
that dimmer planets hide
do the bats know
can they see better
or cry their little
tweet-cries to tell
the unseen moths
from moonbeams
just what are moonbeams
and why is Jupiter so bright
is he jealous
of the period-making
sea tide-breaking
mother
that caused the first counting
it's been this many moons
I'm this many moons
and this many moons from now
how the oysters break
when to know to give
and when to take

STARS

Stars like glowing

                Plankton

in a dark Sea
galaxies Sargasso –
Flotsum of gas and matter

                Turbulant

They say the universe turns round itself
Being itself

                Round

Curves to meet itself –

            If I go forward

Relentless and straight
will I end up where I am or was

            Here ?

If I stop a moment to rest
are a thousand years

            Lost ?

REALMS OF LIGHT

Lucid the realms of light
in sleeping hours
true to heart
and simple
they become
pure dreams and
all the powers of night
cannot rise against them

DOORS AND WINDOWS

the doors and windows are all opened now
the cat's not surprised
the summer's been so long she's grown
there's the occasional wren that comes up
to the sliding screens
and the monarchs are headed back
if they make it through the traffic
they'll stay above the crime
the air is different now
and there'll be seeds to sow
rocket and parsley and rye

WORDS

are words
to memories
like
pinpoints of light
to stars thousands of miles across
greater than earth
and so far away
we only see them at night
when the air of thought
is clear?

Humanity

BREATHE IN BREATHE OUT

the first thing we do is
breathe in
and then we have this life
and all the stuff that makes it life
or that's what we call it
and then we breathe out

HELLO!

Cataracts torn from tearing eyes
Gauze of a million lives
Dissolving on something so simple as
Breath!

LAST NIGHT I HEARD THAT
FERLINGHETTI WAS STILL ALIVE

Last Night I heard that Ferlinghetti was still
Alive
which is like hearing that Jesus was still alive
But
Really alive not Ascended into
Space
but down here
Breathing our minds
and expelling words
Like
Caravaggio brush strokes

SMALL THINGS IN ITALY

It was the small or smaller things
not St. Mark's or
St. Peter's
they were big enough for anybody
but to a twenty-one year old
the graffiti in the piazzas
a good gelato
a drunk American girl staggering around
the Italians smirking
the way they trimmed the pines
a piece of brick off the Colosseum
and meekly opening some
big side doors at St. John Lateran
and peeking inside and
the guide at that moment saying
"…and these were the doors
of the Roman Senate"
and St. Cecilia in a sari
the Forum cats fed by an old lady
or before the vandal hit
how I touched Jesus' Pietá foot
fern growing out of Pompeii walls
ancient columns as stands for potted plants
the long train trip to Calabria
some guys speaking Greek
but I didn't know it yet

hill towns perched high above
artichoke gardens
picnics on promontories
above Scilla and Charibdis
the smell of the sacred
smoke going up to the gods as always
those eerie nightfalls
and thousand year old olive trees
or how stone steps could be worn down
by feet for centuries

THEY BELIEVE IN ANGELS NOW

he of the iron ore
smelted
she of the
lost family
milk and vinegar
they never mixed
till now and they
are old and afraid
they cling against
the inevitable
sting of death
and worse
loneliness
kids grown
they believe in angels now

BIBLIOPHILES

I'm in the Bookstore
AGAIN
Wandering mind fully
Stack slumming
Finding a lucious little
Beat anthology
And hurry to the checkout
Quickly, stealthily like some
Bum who's just found a
Diamond ring in the gutter
Even clutching it to my chest
I hand it to the clerk
She fondles it from my hand
"Ooh this has a nice FEEL"
She says (Lasciviously?)
"Yes, doesn't it" I answer
"You LOVE books too" I say
And wink invisibly,
She lets out a "Yes"
That's almost Joycean—
"Yes, I do........."
We say LOVE
but does she know
What I know,
That when we say love
We mean FETISH
And would she blush to hear that?
"Ever been to City Lights in San Francisco?"
"You'd LOVE it" I say
                    Did I hear her sigh?

POLIO WEATHER

Stay inside and play
she said
It's Polio weather
which meant it was hot
and kids were ending up in iron lungs
which was a lot worse than
playing in your room all day
and swimming pools were deadly
that's where the germs were
from unknown vectors
in the splashing water
or was it the wind
or the food
so we stayed inside and watched TV
old movies were our friends
and we knew our actors
davis crawford bogart lorie
the maltese falcon
and the songs from
casablanca
ate crackerjacks
and got little prizes in every box
we watched the saucers land
in basic black and white
chilled to hear the words

People of the Planet Earth
we come in Peace
but we knew they were communists
and didn't come in peace
said the Angelus when evening fell
or the Rosary by the window
saw the stars gleaming
the sycamores leaning
against the breeze
and slept beneath cool sheets

FATIGUES

Today at lunch
with my everything bagel and a bit of ham
and tea
I shared a table with two soldiers
in fatigues
they chatted together
about how good the fruit salad was
and what a water chestnut was
we exchanged pleasantries
of strangers in a crowded cafe
and I read about ancient stones
and mysterious animals
my usual light reading and when
their lunch was over the older sergeant got up
and the fresh-faced one stayed a moment to finish his
coke
and I asked
if he'd been "over there yet"
and he said
he was just deployed to Afghanistan
for the first time
so I patted him on the back
and said
"take care of yourself man"
and
"I'll remember you in my prayers"
which is what he might understand better
than the giving and receiving
of breath I would do for him every day
and he smiled and thanked me
and turned to leave
and then I turned to look out the window

OLD SHIRT

I still have
an old batik shirt
twenty years or so
it's beautiful and green
and bold and worn out so
I had to do a bad sew-up job
on the rip under the pocket
but I can sleep in it now
and the buttons
come undone
bum-like
soft
!

YOUNG RACCOON

I heard this crying from a pine
in my garden
sad enough to know it wasn't a bird
I checked and
saw a young raccoon
he'd been weaned
maybe too early
or not
I don't know that much
coonology
but he looked at me
crying a while
then loped off growling
and big enough to raid garbage
he's been around every night
looking in and envying
my spoiled cat
at three in the morning
wanting food
breaking plants
turning over pots
and making all kinds of mistakes
to get on with his life
after his mom abandoned him
to what ruff fate

I should call to have him trapped
but he's already trapped
by life
the heat
and desperation
he wants to live like
anybody
if I feed him he won't go away
if I don't, he's on his own

COYOTE ON THE EDGE

On the ever leading
ledge of time
I wrote the line
that sat like a lump of loneliness on that
cushions edge
coming as it does in a haze of thought
and thoughtlessness
the breath cools and vaporizes the
out and out and out
to space and beyond
and coming again as to does to the
warp of space
and woof of form
the feeling reeling
in a web of
perception
the mitosis
and myosis
of conception
immaculate till
looking down the
coyote cartoon canyon a mile deep
the panic of recognition
seizes the heart in a way
never new
or surprising
the enterprising It
awakes and makes itself anew

MAX

i saw him as my little truck turned
onto my street and
almost in the front yard
the september light caught
his fur so there was no doubting
and i pulled over and naturally went straight for
him
and he stopped and i stopped and called to
him and the red collar gave
away somebody was
keeping him but now he
was on his way away
he didn't care just away and he was peeing on
every tree to mark the
escape
he'd never make
so i called him over and he loped around me
but not up to me and not
afraid and i fed him bacon
bits from the fridge and
hoped he'd never go but at
last
they came for him and they said his name
was max and yes he was a
wolf

ROADTRIP

we didn't know we couldn't do it
three other guys and me
i only had seventy-five bucks
to last me two weeks
but we did it because
we didn't know we couldn't do it
so we saw the grand canyon
and tuscon
and lights of vegas from a distance
then southern california
and we went to disneyland
saw marilyn's legs in cement
and found out the pacific
was cold not like our gulf
i bought incense in some
little chinese store
and burned it for years
and still use the brand
we didn't know
we couldn't do it
we were too young
not to know the
possible

BAT

At first it looked like a dead leaf
Maybe from a sycamore
Moldy and webbed looking
Not grey
Not brown
Just mousey
And clinging
To the side of the house
Just under the eave—
Then it moved
A little shudder at first
Then more
Then it stretched
And the boy saw
Its bat wings unfold

CHILIPETÍN

Like a chili's first bite
Waking up
The mind
Enjoy a delectable feast
Offering to
Deities
Large and small.
The teacher's
There

Earth

HORSEBACK

sit straight in the saddle
gaze over his soft horse ears
eyes ahead resting
on distant mountains

CHIMAYÓ

the trip there is pleasant enough for us
a few climbs and slides down hills
in a fragrant valley
as I remember it
the place where red velas are sold
but I already bought one in Santa Fe
then the short drive to the Santuario
the acequia out front flowing with cold spring water
he'll sit next to this and find the healing here
—I go inside
the church filled with all the Catholic stuff
and to the left a room full of
pictures and canes and cards
and thank you for this and thank you for that
—the usual things of sickness
or uncertain death
I wait my turn to go through the little door
and while I wait
a woman with a little baseball capped kid browned
by chemo - she grips him tight and
guides him through the door –
then out after a while, he's got dirt on his shy
little bald head
next a well dressed matron her black hair
done up she's all classy and she's still
but when she comes out her eyes are flowing dusty tears –
then my turn and through the door

I light my vela take off my shoes
and sit in front of the crucified christ
the pozo full of last nights added dirt
and fill a small jar with some for home
I stick my painful feet into the hole
the window to the right lets in New Mexico light
and pain is gone—
then through the door again—
it's the old man on crutches turn
to let the dirt do its work

THE MULE DEER HERD

i clunked on my boots
in the cabin trying to not awaken the
other guys and
as usual not too good at it
so i walked out into that fifteen-below
front-range morning
and on to the trail to downtown
crunching the crusty snow
and frosty mud
gradually downward
till i caught up with the
mule deer herd—
they were calm and i was all
meditated so i was inside
them and we weren't afraid
and they breathed clouds of
deer breath on me and the
does got a little between me and
the yearling fawns
then stopping they all looked left toward
towering rocks and sniffed and we knew
we were being watched

BUBBLES IN A STREAM

the stream
an eddy in the stream
a whirling turbulent
refuge
a centrifuge
a mass of bubbles spinning
jostling each other
as if the whole of space were finite
the bubbles unite
separate
reunite
penetrate
and burst
for a moment and then
ultimately return
to the flow
the stream

EDNA ST. VINCENT MILLAY

Edna St. Vincent Millay
I think about you
every day
Your name
begins to stick
in a way
Edna
Edna
Etna—a volcano in Sicily
that periodically
Blows its top for two thousand years
They march saints to your summit
to make the lava stop
St. Vincent
St. Vincent
A tropical island in the Caribbean
Idyllic, peaceful
But wait
Isnt there another volcano
nearby?
I think of you blowing your top
On the beach
Another volcano
Periodically spewing lava
Millay
Millay

Malaise sets in
A condition of chronic fatigue
From exploding volcanos and
I think that I shall never see
You
without your top
On the beach
I cannot make it stop
Edna St. Vincent Millay

LATE AUGUST LIGHT

What is it about this late August light
the angle and the warmth of it
but not the burning heat
from just a week before
especially when it comes
from the southwest
and hits the car window
or the sidewalk
or sparkles on the leaves of
july exhausted trees
or zinnias gone to seed
or a trail of ants on the ground
in the evening but not so late
that August light
just before the rain starts
and the breeze stiffens at night
whispering in my ears
and before the crickets chime
and before school starts
yes that's the light
the low angled light
the goldfish tone
it's always there
year after year
and makes me
something
not quite
sad

TOMATO HORN WORM

at first the chewed tomato leaves
gave him away
he left the evidence on
the bottom of the pot
then the half-eaten tomatoes left
to rot
he's huge
as big as my thumb
and he's armed with
biting spray
what can I do now
but let him stay
and mutate into
what?
I want to see
what butterfly
he'll be

AUTUMN NOT GOODBYE

The angled light
has come again
to honeycomb hills
and lengthened shadows
reach dark fingers
to feel where you have walked

Though geese and cranes could
show the way
don't follow them
but stay the short
winter—
the water never freezes here!

ELEGY

Summer has overspent itself
And the pale flowers
Of cedar elms drift down
Their hidden glory among the branches
Past in mere hours
They compost barren ground

SUMMER

the rain comes timid at first
then in squalls
in fits and starts
then falls
steadily and begins to fill
the low spots and run
like a little river
down the walks
the back of summer
broken

PRAIRIE

the past is so secret
when viewed through
tear-filled eyes
it hides like a distant prairie
there but for the
details
the grasses and herbs unclear
and blending
seasonally golden green or
heat seared brown
their species
uncertain
flowers, seed heads, stalks
overgrown
and entangled
here and there a fragrant sage
or is it a spikey yucca
or a cow?
then let the wind-driven snow
cover it all
till it shimmers
blue-white in the sun

SLUGS ON A WINTER NIGHT

nights breath hangs
silent cold vapor
wets the bricks
slugs delight

TO TARA AND THE VIRGIN MARY

Om Taré
Tu Taré
Turé Swaha
Green and perky breasted
how like and unlike
your fellow queen
of Heaven.
you smelling of earth
and moistness
and spring heaving
of life-sitting on the moon-on-a-lotus
Right leg extended
and she in white and blue
a modest
Barbie-schicksa
smelling of
not too expensive cologne
riding on clouds
held aloft by
corpulent putti
is she jealous?

EARTH

I think that dirt has saved my life
the mysterious substance
the medicine of the Earth Herself
I wash Her skin off my skin and
once again she and I have healed ourselves

Lou Faiel-Dattilo

Born on the shore of Lake Erie, amid the vinyards, berry farms and now extinct steel plants, he moved with his parents to his mother's native San Antonio, Texas during the Fifties. He attended Catholic schools from kindergarten through college, where he disturbed his teachers with his interest in Eastern religions and a propensity to sit in full lotus posture whenever he had the chance.

His first remembered television program was the coronation of Queen Elizabeth II and he subsequently watched the McCarthy hearings and Yankee baseball games with his father. His hobbies and interests include art, gardening, birdwatching, growing cacti and anthropology.

He lives with his partner of 32 years in Austin, Texas along with a comic-genius cat who thinks she's a black Lab.

He enjoys science fiction, British comedies and mysteries, speaks several (Earth) languages and can't resist cracking a joke.

www.ingramcontent.com/pod-product-compliance
Lightning Source LLC
Chambersburg PA
CBHW071024040426
42443CB00007B/928